Your A+ Legal Office

"The Business of Legal"

Solo and Small Law Firms

Ashley J. Spurgeon

 ISBN: 9798635326282

Table of Contents

Welcome to the A+ Legal Office. This book is written for Lawyers because that is the field I have most enjoyed. This information can easily transfer to any service-based business.

I have spent my whole life in customer service, front office management, and small businesses of my own or for others. I do know that I have become an expert. I also have my fields of study in marketing, management, and psychology. I have been working with the public since my first job as a 16-year-old high school student. Every job I had, they would put me on the phones and front desk because I have such a good phone voice and personable customer service style. I have run my own businesses (Some successful and others not so much). I had a web design company for ten years with clients from coast to coast. I was a real estate agent with great success. I learned organization skills from being a mother and running a household. I have worked as a counselor and ran a residential drug rehab. I have worked in marketing, sang in my church choir, and volunteered for Habitat for Humanity, where I worked on fundraising on the board of directors in Lawrenceburg, TN. I have had a vibrant and fulfilling professional life. And a great personal experience as well. I have also been a waitress, receptionist, office manager, bookkeeper, the list goes on. My current boss just laughs and asks, "What haven't you done?"

I am also an author, speaker, and personal and business coach and consultant, mother of 4, a wife, and mom to my "Fur Baby" Dom a beautiful German Shepherd. I live in the Houston area and love it. Everything is green year-round. What is not to love? Why am I writing this book? Everywhere I go, conventions, networking events, my doctor's office, I am asked advice on how to improve the functioning of people's office staff and management. I have been giving free advice for so long, and it just does not make sense. I am currently working as the Director of Marketing and Front Office Manager for a Houston Bankruptcy law firm. When I first started there, we would have maybe 3 or 4 people scheduled for the next day consultations now we are booked at least 2-weeks out. I spent 30-minutes in my driveway one weekend talking with a struggling attorney. He had a solo practice that just cost him money and now works for another firm, but the feeling in the office is not the most comfortable. After talking for a little while, he went home and wrote back that if I ever start consulting, he will hire me in an instant to come in and help create the business that leads to a successful firm. I thought to myself...."Why am I just giving away my hints, experience, and advice?"

I still work at a successful law firm in Houston, Texas, as I write this book, but I am also an author, speaker, and life/business coach with my own practice. The fantastic thing is that I can do all of that and still enjoy what life has to offer. I spend time with my family, we eat together every night, and I have time to pursue my passions and purpose.

I write to help others achieve the same dream. You can have the goal of a 40-hour workweek, travel without being digitally connected to your firm, attending the special events in your children's lives without sacrificing your firm or profits.

Learning to work smarter, not harder; you can grow your practice while learning to enjoy your life. You are starting with having the best staff and moving to streamline your practice, all stemming from a clear vision of what you want for your life both professionally and personally. I hope you enjoy what I share. Please contact me with your questions. **ashleyjspurgeon@gmail.com** or **https://www.ashleyjspurgeon.com/**

Dedication

First, I want to say a BIG thank you to J. Thomas Black, Attorney at Law. I have learned so much from you in our time together. 6+ years at your firm have been so enjoyable. I wish you the best of retirement.

To the Staff of the Law Office of J Thomas Black; Alex, Rob, Lorinda, Stephanie and Eddie. You all are a shining example of the A+ Team. I wish you all the best in your new endeavours. It was a fun 6+ years.

Sean Daley of the Rainmaker Institute. You have been a wonderful cheerleader and gave great input to the excerpts I sent your way. Thank you for your encouragement and enthusiasm to make this book happen.

My Family, all your love, support, and encouragement to keep going and create the dream life. Todd, Michael, Sasha, Erin, Rachel, Sue, Sandy, and My Daddy. I would not be who I am today with out al of you.

Part 1: The Work Environment

CHAPTER 1: Introduction

You have a solo firm, small business, or just want to improve what is already in place. Do you know that no matter how big your dreams are, your staff can "Make or Break" your business? You could have spent years in school, networking, and building your dream practice just to find you have few clients, unhappy customers, or high staff turnover. How do you get off the treadmill?

The staff you have in your office can make a big difference. I know it seems obvious that these people are the first and most often contact with the people who will be or are your clients. If you have the wrong people in place, it can have a detrimental effect on your success.

We will discuss the core values you are looking for when hiring an A+ team, how to market yourself and your business to bring success to your field and how to organize your front office and staff so that you do not have to worry about them. They will be a well-oiled machine that does not need your constant supervision.

As I said, I am an expert in the field. I have dedicated my life, 30+ years, to learning, studying, and implementing so that people can have the great experience of enjoying what they do, and have pride in what they have spent years building. Cherishing the clients you have, having a cohesive team, and getting great reviews for being a remarkable firm or practice that changes people's lives. Not only that but to make the money you have dreamed of.

What do you want more than that? How about a staff that is so reliable and proficient that you can take extended vacations and know you can come home to a smoothly running firm? Doesn't that sound like a dream? It is a dream that can become a reality. I am here to help that dream manifest into reality.

In a law office, employees should step into the office running. My philosophy is "on time is 5-minute late". As soon as I get to my desk I am working. I plow through my tasks and projects every day, one after another, until everything is complete. When my boss asks me to do something it is completed right away. My inbox is empty every night when I go home, both the physical one and email. Anticipating the needs of my boss and handling them before asked is essential to me. Looking for ways to improve the functioning of the firm and save or make money is a priority. And believe it or not, I get all of this done in a 40-hour workweek. I will share here how to accomplish this.

I love my job. I have been there 6+-years, and I still love it. What makes my job so great? I believe in what we do. We genuinely help people achieve a new start in life. We provide help and answers to problems. My boss has a high level of integrity and honesty as a person and in practice. I have so much respect for him and who he is as a lawyer and a person. Everything in business does start at the top and trickles down. We are honest with our clients and honest in our time billing. We produce results, and each year I see our firm growing financially.

You will know what to look for and how to structure a practice to see these fantastic results. Know it takes time and patience, and a lot of work on everyone's part of making this happen. By learning from experience, you can achieve this dream practice in a lot less time.

Thank you for joining me on this adventure. I know that at this point, you have already spent thousands trying different ideas and techniques, most failing.

The goal here is to help you succeed and not have to worry about the office again. Just enjoy that your first contact ambassadors, and the rest of your staff, are allowing you to do what you always wanted to do. You do not have to spend so much time worrying over the "Business" end of your firm or office.

We will also take time to look at the cohesion between the front and back offices, and broach the subjects of your life outside of work, and how to not just survive dynamic changes in business but to thrive in them as well.

Let's Enjoy the Ride,
Ashley J Spurgeon

"You work to live….
Not Live to Work"

Chapter 2: What is your Business Structure?

When you went to school to be what you are, a lawyer, chances are you learned about your trade and ethics, but not much focus on business. You have already discovered you cannot get your degree, hang your shingle, and people will just call you or walk through your door. You cannot only have one case settlement and a good client review, and people will flock to your door or flood your phone with calls. You need to have some business knowledge. Managing the business can take up a lot of your time and take away from the time you need to build the firm or office you dreamed of having and practicing law. If you wanted to be a business manager, you would have taken business management in college instead. The fact, though, is that you must be a business manager while creating the perfect practice. At the same time, you can have people on staff who will gladly take this end off your hands and follow your dream, bring in your business and not scare off potential clients.

At the same time, you can have a personal life. Being able to go to your children's events, nurture the relationship with your partner, taking a vacation without your cell phone or laptop always within reach. Doesn't that sound too good to be true? I am going to show you how to make this dream a reality.

When asking, "What is your business structure," we are not talking about the sole proprietor, LLC, PC Corporation. We are discussing the underlying bare bones of your office and staff itself. What is the structure of your office? Are you genuinely solo and doing all the work yourself? Do you have a small team to help you get the job done? Are you a small to medium office with multiple personalities?

There are essential steps you need to lay down, your foundations. I teach these concepts and help you develop them in my personal consulting. But we will touch on the different areas.

Do you have a business plan on paper? The business plan is the road map for your future if you want to succeed. I am not talking about the detailed financial and marketing business plan. I am talking about how you and your employees work together. How do you develop and maintain the relationships with your potential, current, and past clients? You want to grow, but what is your vision? Usually, it is to be able to have enough income to be able to enjoy your family and your life outside of work. We will talk about a work-life balance later.

Here are some points for you to ponder.
What are your core values?
What is your business structure?
Who are your ideal clients?
Who are your ideal employees?
Do your employees know your mission?
Can your employees tell you what the core values are?
Are they aligned with them?
What do you bring to the marketplace that sets you apart from the crowd?
What is your marketing plan?
How do you create and keep an A+ Team?
What are your processes and procedures?

How is your business office structured? I know you are the boss. You earned this right with your years at college, your financial investment, your expertise in the field, and your reputation. You are the boss, but do you want to be the one who must handle every personality conflict or employee training, on-boarding, and the mess of office politics?

The thing about small firms and offices, many times job tasks and responsibilities overlap. They just must, to get everything done. But it is still essential to have a defined structure or chain of command. If you do not, every conflict or problem that arises gets dumped in your lap.

Here is an example. We have the owner, and then we have the front office and back office. It is nice to know that there is someone to speak to about disagreements or conflicts. We want to do that before having to take them to the "Big Boss." Each section of the office has one designated person to oversee and run the day to day functions, but also to go to when someone needs something. Having someone to resolve conflict takes the weight off the shoulders of the chief decision-maker in the office. You. Do you know that every interruption takes approximately 23 minutes to recover? If you charge $200 per hour for your services that is almost $100 of your time to handle a conflict or situation that could have been handled by someone else, at about $30 per hour.

In a small firm or office, things tend to be a little more relaxed than in a large corporation or business. But for the sake of keeping the peace and things running smoothly, it is a good idea to have someone in the front office and someone in the back office, which can be delegated as the one to talk to when there is a problem.

Being a “type A” personality can lead to trying to do everything yourself so that it gets completed correctly and promptly. Learning to delegate and trust others to do things can be a huge step. Your job is to practice your area of expertise, be sure you have clients bringing in money for you, that the laws and ethics of your practice areas followed, etc.

"Work smarter, not harder."

Enough rhetoric. Let us get down to the bare bones of a great business, staff, and a star office.

Chapter 3: Hiring the RIGHT People

No one likes the hiring process. We recently had our great receptionist move into a paralegal position. We put off her promotion just because she was so good in the front office; we did not want to have to replace her. My boss and I would sit in his office and groan over the thought of resumes, interviews, and how many will we go through before we find another "Good Fit" to our firm culture.

The first thing you must know about hiring for the front office or any position is the following:

If you are not 100% satisfied with who you hired for a job, then let that person go and try again. It takes time to get to know someone. How skilled are they? What is their personality? How organized are they? How do they relate to your clients and their specific needs? How do they react under pressure? You can not know someone from just an interview.

"Hire Slowly & Fire Quickly"

Here is a scenario:

You hire a receptionist, and she is OK. But just OK, not great. You get to know a little about her private life and some of her struggles. You like her, OK, but she is not an excellent fit for your firm. You have a heart and keep saying, let us see if she can grow into the position. I know because I have been in this position more than once. You feel bad that if you let her go, she will have even more setbacks and personal hardships.

Let me give you another thought on this: if she is not the right fit for your office, then keeping her on staff may also be holding her back to find something better for her. Having the wrong person leaves an undercurrent of things not being entirely in place or settled in the office. The confidence is never wholly established in the position.

If you want an A+ team, then you must make the hard choices right when you know you need to make them. It is not personal; it is your business. How you make your money and support your family. If you know you can do better, then strive for the better. Hire slowly and fire quickly.

I know turnover is difficult. The time taken from other staff members for training alone is stressful and time-consuming, not to mention expensive. But having the wrong person in place can hinder the productivity of the other staff members, lose you clients, and just create more work for yourself or others. Keep trying until you find the right person. Later we will discuss putting policies and procedures in place to make a turnover much smoother.

Also, keep in mind that the people you hire, you need to like, feel comfortable with, and enjoy spending time with these people. We spend more waking hours with our co-workers than our families.

No one likes the hiring process. It is so easy to give up and SETTLE for someone with the right skills just to eliminate the interruption in business. Or you find someone with the right look and personality, but they do not have the skill set needed.

Here are some hiring suggestions.

Let the office manager handle the weeding out of resumes. They can bring you the 3-5 favorites and they can conduct the first interviews.

1) The online job placement ad.

When placing an online ad for a position, ask 3 to 5 questions that must be answered. They can be simple questions.

- Why would you be considered a star team member?
- What skills will you bring to our office?
- What was a stressful situation, and how did you solve it?
- Also, ask for a cover letter.

The whole idea is that the questions get answered. When we do this, out of 100 applicants, maybe 2 or 3 follow the directions. If someone cannot follow instructions in the application process, how are they going to follow directions on the job? Experience has shown that most people will not provide a cover letter even when asked. This process will weed out almost all the resumes you have to go through. Be sure to check spelling and grammar. If they cannot be correct in a cover letter and resume, which they can take time to perfect, how will your emails and memos appear?

2) Have the first interview over the phone.

Let your office manager or hiring manager have a conversation with this person over the phone. Your front office staff will spend quite a bit on time on the phone with prospective clients and current clients. Working on the phone is a talent, not a teachable skill. When they have the office interview, hand the prospect a script and have them answer a few calls.

We hired a receptionist once that was a nice enough girl. She was educated, articulate but had a voice that, no matter what, sounded unfriendly over the phone. Well, even face to face. It was just the sound of her voice, not anything that could have been fixed or trained. But the fact was that one thing made her wrong for the job. She just could not sound friendly and empathetic on the phone. You may ask why we hired her? She was a family member of one of our staff, whom we all loved and respected.

Now, we come to my next point:

3) Do not hire family members.
You like the person in your office who is asking if you will interview their family member. They are great at their job and good with your clients, so why not give it a shot? Try out the family member they are asking you to hire?

Having a family member in the office brings a whole new dynamic to the office, especially if they are not the right fit for the job. When you need to correct, discipline, or even fire this person, you now must take into consideration both people. Family members tend to be defensive of each other. If you must let one go, it affects both not just professionally but also personally. Hiring a family member is just a situation that is better to avoid.

What happens if there is a family emergency? These do come up. When something happens in a family, then you will have two employees affected and likely out of the office, instead of just one employee absent, you have two.

4) When interviewing, look for more than just skills or personality.

In a busy office, you do not have time to teach necessary office skills. Do not assume that since these young adults grew up on computers since they were three years old that they know how to type, use a 10-key, or work with Microsoft products. Give a few tests to see how they use your equipment. Have them answer the phone, type an email, add some figures. There are certain aspects to any company you will need to teach based on the programs you use. But the necessary skills need to be there, so you have a quicker flow into the position.

Personality is not a teachable skill. In a front office environment, you need someone who is commanding enough to control a phone conversation and yet empathetic to relay a feeling of caring to the prospective client. Do you think it is easy to get people to come in and speak with a lawyer? People are afraid of lawyers. I spend a lot of my time on the phone with people making them feel comfortable with me and the idea of speaking with my boss. Caring and empathy is a talent, not a learned skill. If someone has the right personality, it can be trained to a degree, but for the most part, it needs to be something that comes naturally. You need to seek a level of EQ, Emotional intelligence.

The new hire for a front office needs both skill and personality. If you have a small firm or practice, have several in your staff visit with the interviewee. If anyone has a red flag, then move on to the next prospect. Hiring is not easy or fun but bringing the wrong person on board can set your firm back, lose your clients, and cost you money.

If you hire someone just because they can do a job, your opportunity for them will soon become "Just a Job."

But if you hire people who believe in the vision of the organization, like you, they will work consistently with passion, commitment, resilience, and a positive attitude.

Ty Howard
CEO and Editor in Chief
MOTIVATION Magazine

Chapter 4: What is in a Name?

The other day I was listening to our receptionist on the phone, and she told the caller that she was the secretary. I was thinking, "No, you are the receptionist." Then I thought, did she get a promotion?

The receptionist and a secretary have similar duties in the front office at a small firm, but they are still vastly different. Usually in education and experience. Does this seem a little picky to you? You are probably thinking there is no harm in her calling herself a secretary. How happy will you be when she comes asking for the salary of an experienced secretary with only one year of work experience under her belt?

Different titles come with varying rates of pay. Today's workers are smart and do their research. There is a difference between a receptionist and a secretary. Just as there is an intake specialist and a marketing director, a legal assistant and a paralegal, an associate, and a partner. Names and titles hold power and come with different levels of responsibility. Titles also come with a different price tag for you, the business owner.

When speaking to a client or prospective client, you may want to build their trust in your team member by telling them your receptionist is "your legal assistant." If she overhears this, you should be ready to give her a raise. In her mind, you have also just given her a promotion.

I began my journey in small law firm practice as a part-time intake specialist. Now I am the front office manager and marketing director. I got there by my years of experience, furthering my education, and proving to my boss that I had increased the firm's productivity and helped make him money. I had the facts to prove that my position was worth paying more. But I was not just handed a title; I earned it.

If you are financially ready to give someone a promotion and a raise, then do it. We want to be able to reward our employees for their excellent work and for contributing to the firm. We want to have patriots and not mercenaries, those who only show up only for the paycheck. If you are giving someone a title they are not entitled to, or you do not need someone in that position, you may find yourself backed into a corner because that is the title you have been calling them, and they have heard it.

In a small firm, it is OK to call your receptionist a receptionist. That is her duty and responsibility. You do not need another legal assistant, but if she hears you calling her Legal Assistant, she may just very well ask for that pay grade. Can you afford it, and are you prepared? Is she willing to take on the greater responsibilities of a harder, more demanding role in the law firm? So, I ask you once more, "What is in a name?"

"The Beginning of wisdom is to call things by their right names."

Proverb

Chapter 5: The Onboarding Process

Once again, we are talking about a step that takes time away from you and your staff. If you miss out on the importance of the on-boarding process, you can have trouble down the road.

People coming into your office need to receive information pertinent to your office. You might think that just covering these basics in a conversation is good enough. You are wrong. When it comes to staff discipline or even letting someone go, you might regret skipping essential steps that will save you down the road. Everything needs to be in writing, and every staff member needs to sign that they have read and understood them. Even when you update, have everyone read and sign.

The hiring process is complete, and you have a new employee starting. As a small firm, it is easy to have someone begin and just throw them into the position with simply basic training and HOPE they learn the rest by osmosis. You and your team have, most likely, gotten behind on your work, and you are ready to pull back and breathe a sigh of relief that you no longer must cover a vacant position. It is easy to miss most of the onboarding process, and this can cause problems down the road.

You need to take the time to perform a complete orientation. You need to take time to put everything down in writing, so you do not miss anything. You must also get a signature that everything was read and understood. I know I am repeating myself, but this is important.

Some of the details that need to be in the on-boarding (orientation) process:

1. The proper tax documents and ID.
2. Direct deposit information for pay.
3. An employee handbook
4. Position responsibilities and detailed job description
5. Attendance policy
6. Complete procedure guide for every task
7. Holidays, sick time, personal days, bereavement, and vacation time.
8. Advancement procedures and policies

9. Behavior policies
10. Dress code
11. Termination procedures
12. Online and technology use procedures.
13. Confidentiality and non-compete agreements
14. Communicating with potential and current clients
15. Personal device use (Tables, phones, etc.) in the office.

Part of our consultation package will help you to develop your onboarding process and the needed paperwork and documentation that goes along with it. We are coming from the understanding that your expertise is in your field of law and not business management.

You will need to spend some time on this at least once to create all of this. The on-boarding process seems like a lot of work, but you will not hear later that an employee let go was not informed of a policy. You can refer to the information they signed and agreed to at the start of their employment.

Of course, this is all the C.Y.A stuff. You want someone to be welcomed into your firm to feel appreciated. Start with a friendly, clean workstation. Let them know about how they can personalize and make it their own. Have the welcome packet ready, an onboarding gift—a supply list of items they may need. Make them feel welcomed to the firm. They know that small firms are tight groups that have often been working together for years. It is no fun feeling like the newbie or outsider.

Have one person dedicated to the on-boarding process. They need to be familiar with all the policies, procedures, and paperwork involved.

Soon we will discuss the way to arrange all the policies and procedures, so you only must do this once. I am all about being organized and efficient, so everyone is more productive.

"Train people well enough so they can leave, treat them well enough they will not want to."

~ Richard Branson

Chapter 6: Having a Dream Team

The business world has changed dramatically. If you have been in business 30+ years, you may remember the world of hierarchies and the corporate business structure.

The business world has evolved into one of multiple income streams, working side gigs, and entrepreneurs. Everyone is looking for freedom and flexibility. You have people working remotely, employees looking for the perfect company culture, flextime, and great team environments.

If you are from the "Old School" and are struggling to keep things how you know, you might just get left behind in today's highly competitive marketplace. You need to understand what employees are expecting. You also need to know how to create that within your own business. This book is a key to helping you unlock the new way of doing business where you will be most successful. Your team is the key to your success or your failure.

I have built my business around creating success through the people around me. I also understand that if I want to succeed that everything in my world must start with me, and it all trickles down.

I heard a true story of a CEO that hired a coach to help improve their business. When they sat down and had a conversation about company morale and the working culture, they found it was low, turnover was high, and employees were generally unhappy with their jobs.

In the last 3-years, the CEO had not left his office and traveled the halls of his company. He instructed him to go out for a short time every day and just observe his employees. Talk to them and give feedback and find at least one person a day to complement their work.

The most amazing thing happened in this company. Turn-around almost wholly vanished, attendance improved, productivity improved, employee satisfaction improved, and their profits increased.

"People do not quit their job, they quit their bosses."

~ Unknown

Take a moment to think about that and let it sink it.

- How do you communicate with your staff?
- How do you show up every day?
- What are you doing personally to ensure your team enjoys their work environment?
- How is this affecting how your clients feel or show up?
- Do you love the work you do, and does it show within your organization?

Half of the battle is having the right people in place, which we will look at in the next chapter. The other half is personal work with yourself and how you are showing up in your own life.

Honestly, people are terrified of having to call an attorney. Since you work this day in and day out, you might forget this.

They are, first off, in a bad life situation. If they were not, they would not need you. But what they are afraid of is having to work with a lawyer and their staff. The reputation is shady dealings, questionable practices, poor communication, and fraudulent billing. Prospective clients have already experienced trauma or tragedy. They are afraid of being taken advantage of by those who have promised to serve them.

There is the keyword. TO SERVE.

Are you and your team working in a service mindset, or have you been doing this one thing for so long the business of law has become just getting people in, filed, and then successfully discharged or receive a settlement; then on to the next one.

The law field is a service industry. We will also talk more about this coming up.

"Teamwork makes the dream work, but a vision becomes a nightmare when the leader has a big dream and a bad team."

~ *John C. Maxwell*

Chapter 7: The Attributes of an A+ Team

We have already talked about hiring the best people for the job and letting go of those that are not a perfect fit. But who are the ideal team members, and how can you identify them? These are people who have very particular traits and not always easy to find. Once found, they must be nurtured. Of course, this starts from the top down. Do you have the attributes of an A+ team member?

First, let us look at what those are and what the attributes are.

Impact

People with impact are those who want to leave a lasting impression on those they encounter. They encourage people to be their best. Encouragement is not just with co-workers but your clientele also. These are the encouragers. It cannot be false praise. It comes from the heart. People feel sincerity.

Patriots, not mercenaries.

Does your staff love what they do? Do they love coming to work, showing up with smiles and positive attitudes? Do they show up on time and ready to dive into their day? I have heard it said that when people love what they do, they are "Patriots." If they are just working for money, they are "mercenaries." Who do you want in your office? Patriots are loyal, hardworking, and have empathy for those they are working with, the clients, and their co-workers. Patriots are those who believe in your vision, serving people, and they will be your top advocates.

A mercenary is just that. A mercenary receives pay from doing a job, collect the paycheck, and go home. These types of employees also have a higher turnover rate because they are looking for the greener pastures and/or the higher pay. They do not share your vision or have a passion for what you do.

Have a growth Mindset

Does your staff have a desire to grow your business? Are they just coming in and doing what is expected of them every day? There are qualities to people with a growth mindset.

- They embrace their flaws
- They see failures as an opportunity
- They see criticism as constructive

- They focus on growth versus outcomes.

Excellence: Dignity, pride, and personal Excellence

These are the people who take pride in their work. Even mundane tasks are completed exceptionally well. They want to do things not for praise but because they know they have done their best.

Humility

I have heard it defined best as not thinking less of yourself but thinking of yourself LESS. I believe that is a good point. Those who are altruistic, giving and kind, putting others first, and taking responsibility for themselves are rare finds and worth holding on to. The qualities of a team player with humility are as follows:

- Naturally puts others first
- Shine the spotlight on others
- Leads by example
- Takes personal responsibility for themselves and does the right thing.
- Admits their mistakes - Be real
- Asks questions instead of making statements

- Really listens
- Let others do their job instead of micromanaging
- Has a sense of humor

Hunger

These are people with desire. They have the drive to want more out of life. They WANT to grow and work to be better. These are the people who look for new frontiers, not only to be great but to lead others to greatness.

Smart: Not IQ but EQ (Emotional Intelligence)

These are the people with a natural sense of empathy. They know how to walk in another's shoes and can hear what is not said. Their attributes are:

- They handle impulse, reactions, and responses.
- They can handle difficulties and setbacks.
- They can handle pressure, stress, and intensity.

Extreme Ownership

- Taking 100% responsibility in 100% of everything they do in their lives.
- They take ownership by accepting:
- They recognize and act on what they did and what they did not do but should have
- 100% responsible for how they react to what happens to them.

A "Do it Now" mindset

These people are the opposite of procrastinators, and they act with spark speed. If there is a client or associate who is challenging to get in touch with, the task will be given to that person because they can get someone on the phone within, usually, 5-minutes. When presented with a task, it is taken care of right away, and they have systems in place for themself so that it is not put off or forgotten.

I know that when a boss asks me to do something, I cannot say, "no, I won't do that," but if I see that someone else should do it because they will do a better job, then I speak up. Do not ask your employees who take on too much. They need to have enough leeway to feel comfortable to say I cannot do this and come with a suggestion of how that task can be better managed. Quite easy to do when you work in a small firm. But if you have an employee who is really at their limit of what they can do in their allotted time, they need to feel comfortable speaking up. Trying to do too much will make an employee less productive and leave room for more mistakes.

Reliable (The rarest trait): Handling your "stuff." They are being counted on to follow through without follow-up from others. They are also able to anticipate the needs of those who rely on them, ahead of their needs.

- They do not over-promise. Reliable people say if something will not or cannot be completed to your satisfaction.

- Proactively communicate. Do not leave other people hanging. Let people know if things do not go as planned or deadpan.

- Start and Finish - Initiative and closure. Reliable people start strong and finish strong.

- Have pride. A task is completed because they said they would.

Resourceful: Adaptive to change

Change is so rapid, and it is a part of everyday life. We are always learning. If they do not know something, then they figure it out. Resources are now limitless to find what we need to know. Google, YouTube, etc. all have examples and learning tutorials on just about everything. Plus, people in your office may already know.

- Figure it out.
- Who do you know that has dealt with something similar? People love to help.
- Do not steal ideas. Taking ideas from one is plagiarism; taking ideas from many is research.
- Have contingencies.
- Use creative destruction. Break the rules (Think outside the box); make it happen. Make it up until it works.

Constancy: Doing the thing they say they are going to do, long after the mood they said it in leaves them.

When there is a new task or project, it is easy to get excited and jump on the chance to be a part of it. You volunteer yourself in the excitement. Once you start working on it, you now realize that it is difficult or time-consuming.

I do not know how many times I have done this in a desire to help others lessen their load or bring something new to the firm. I have had to creatively find ways to rework my time and priorities to make it happen. I will moan and complain about it later, that is until I figure out how to integrate it into my work week smoothly. I made a promise, and I am determined to keep it. Even when I no longer feel the excitement of the new idea or project.

- Have faith that if you keep working at it, you will see results.

- Once you begin to see results, push through. Things become easier by being consistent. If you stop, you will have to start back at the beginning and push through again. An example is the goal of working out or weight loss.

- Failure occurs because of not sustaining once you see results.

- Lack of consistency is the thief of dreams. The stop and start process kills progress in any pursuit.

If you stay consistent, even slowly, ultimately, you will beat the most talented of competitors

These are the core values of an A+ team. It is not easy to find, but when you do, then you will have an office staff that works very well, encourages each other to be better every day and strives to adapt and grow. These star people have service as the forefront of working with clients and each other.

"The success of teamwork:
Coming together is the beginning
Keeping it together is progress
Working together is success."

~ Henry Ford

CHAPTER 8: Working with Systems

My boss gave me a book to read that was called "*The Power of a System*" by John H. Fisher. He had just finished reading it, and we become a team to place systems to work in our law practice. We created working procedure manuals for every position in the firm. A system allows for smooth transitions in any situation. Think of it this way:

If someone had to leave for an extended period and you needed to bring in a temp worker, how can they quickly know how to do each task for that position. It was not hard to do. I will use my marketing as an example. We do a lot of direct mail campaigns. I opened a Microsoft word document. As I went through the steps from creating a mailing list to stamping the envelope, I placed ever single step down.

We did the same for every task in every position. The receptionist had responsibilities such as answering the phone, and this included the script of what to say—setting appointments, placing appointments on the calendar, entering the new contacts in the CRM database. We listed how to confirm appointments, how to leave voice mails, and the scripts for those.

Every communication has a script so that there is always consistency and professionalism.

We also did this for the paralegals. They will procrastinate and not want to do this, but each task only needs to be written out once, and it does not take a lot of time. It will save you so much time when it comes to someone new needing to do these tasks.

We have letters that go out to clients for specific situations. They have a meeting of creditors; they are discharged from their case; the trustee files a motion to dismiss. As these notices come through, the person responsible for mailing these letters has step-by-step directions that start with which program to use to where to find the letter template, to placing essential dates of the calendar. With these instructions written down, a new hire will be trained that much quicker without having to pull someone else away from their job to explain again.

We also placed every bit of information into a wiki database. If we need to know something, then all we must do is open it up and search by using key terms. Written procedures, for me, is beneficial when someone calls to schedule an appointment, but it is not our area of law. We used to have to flip through a notebook or, even worse, commit to memory some attorneys in different practices to recommend. Now I can search for "Family Law," and we get a list of a few different recommended attorneys. I just copy and paste that list into an email and send it to the person who was looking for help. So, they did not hire our firm, but they might remember the support and kindness, and now is a referral source back to us.

The point of having systems in place is:

1. Work smarter not harder
2. Have smooth transitions for new employees
3. You do not have to be a walking encyclopedia of knowledge. It is at your fingertips.

Everything, every task, every policy with both employees and clients needs to be in writing. It can be bound in notebooks, or you can have an online resource such as a wiki knowledge base. If you do not have it in writing, then you will later hear, "No one ever told me that."

The best way to find yourself
is to lose yourself in the
service of others.

~Gandhi

CHAPTER 9: Hospitality is Key

Even though you are a law office, your clients and potential clients should look forward to coming to see you. Remember, they have put themselves in your care and have invested in you. They should feel welcomed and that your office cares. How are your potential clients brought into your world, and by whom?

Our clients come to us because they have been traumatized and are in pain. They have already most likely tried to cure themselves and failed. Now they are turning to you. They come to you in great need of healing and help. You and your staff are the professions who can bring it to them.

When someone calls the office to ask for help, do they feel like they have come to the right place, or do they think they are interrupting someone?

When the phones get answered, does the person on the other end feel they have the full attention of the person they are speaking? Someone needs to be in this position who has the time and the skills to listen, respond, and put them at ease.

The conversation does not mean a one-hour dialogue.

The intake person knows how to ask a question to determine if this client is a good fit for your firm. He or she knows how to direct the flow of the conversation. Your clients get pre-qualified, and they know what to expect next. Not what they need to do but what they can expect from you and your office that will help them relieve their pain.

Think of the caller as the long-lost friend? You are speaking to them now. When they call is over the potential or current client should feel:

- Heard
- Understood
- Cared about
- Relieved, and
- Hopeful

Is this how people feel after talking with your office? Remember, soon you are going to ask this person to share personal and intimate information. They will be paying a significant amount of money. Do they feel comfortable doing that, or do they feel hesitant?

When someone enters your office, they should feel like an invited guest: not just the first time but every time.

"I'm so glad you made it in to see us."
"I'm happy to meet you."

What phrases do you hear your front office using when someone comes into your office? How they speak to clients is particularly important if you want to build a successful, thriving business.

How do you welcome friends into your home? Do you stop what you are doing and greet them, or do you make them wait until while you continue typing away on your computer? Remember, you invited them, and they should feel as if you are expecting them. Are they greeted by name or asked their name?

If your team acts like each new client is just more work, they have a backward attitude. Of course, they are more work. That is why we want them there. We get paid to produce results. What should relay as feelings and emotions are that we are happy they came in. We have a healing gift to give them. Do they feel like they are in a healing place or a factory?

How we treat our clients from pre-qualification to discharge is critically essential. Do they feel cared about and welcome with every encounter and every phone call? You can be welcoming at stage one then push them through the grinder the rest of the way. That is not the memory of working with you that your past clients should have. You want happy clients even if they do not see the results they are hoping to achieve. They will leave at the end of the service, knowing that you and your staff cared about them, and your team did everything they could to help ease their pain and solve their problems. These are your reviews and referrals down the road or tomorrow. When they talk to other people or post on Google, what will they say about you and your firm? Will it make you or break you?

The success of your firm is dependent on people loving their experience with you and your staff. Are you on track right now to take good care of the people who call and enter your front door?

It does begin with the first phone call. When the potential client calls, how are they greeted on the phone? Do they hear, "Law Office" and left to pick up the conversations? Or do they hear, "Thank you for calling ________, This is ____, How can I help you?

When clients must fill out paperwork, do they get to sit in a clean and comfortable office? Are they offered anything to drink?

I heard of one law firm that has a menu they present to clients. With a Keurig beverage station, they can choose between coffees, teas, and bottled water. Wouldn't this make your ***"Guests"*** feel more welcomed?

When the potential or current client enters a conference room, is there a notepad and pen ready for them to take notes? Taking these small steps may feel like over the top, but it makes people feel like you were anticipating their visit and prepared ahead of time just for them.

You may think, "I'm just a struggling solo practitioner," how can I afford these things? Believe me, if you go an extra step, then you will be able to provide it. You will see your client retention rate increase because they feel cared about and taken care of in one of the scariest times of their lives. When people are happy, they tell their friends about it also. How does that sound?

"A client is the most important visitor on our premises. ***He is not dependent on us****. We are dependent on him.* ***He is not an interruption in our work****. He is the purpose of it.* ***He is not an outsider in our business****. He is part of it.* ***We are not doing him a favor by serving him****. He is doing us a favor by giving us the opportunity to do so"*

~ Mahatma Gandhi

CHAPTER 10: Solo Practitioners – You do not have to work alone.

I admire solo practitioners because they are the most organized. Or they should be. Did that statement make you laugh because you feel anything but organized? You must wear every hat in your solo firm. You are the lawyer, paralegal, receptionist, marketing, intake, bookkeeping, and anything else that needs to be done. You answer the phones, schedule the appointments, hold consultations, retain clients, collect paperwork, do research, file motions, and pleadings, and make the court appearances. WOW! I am exhausted just thinking about it, and I am sure there is more that you do.

With all of this going on, the law is your life. There is no time for more. What about your relationships, kids, social life, personal life, or vacations? Those are either strained or non-existent.

How is your sleep? The few hours you may get. How is your health? Is this what you dreamed of your life to be when you first started law school and envisioned your future?

The first thing you want to do is STOP! Right now! Just for 5-minutes. Turn off your monitor, shut of your phone's sound, take off your shoes, relax into a comfortable chair, and put on some soft music. Now, close your eyes and breathe. Relax for 5-minutes (you can set a timer). When you are done come back to this post.

Do you feel a little better? Or was your mind spinning the whole time about what you should be doing instead of breathing for 5-minutes?

You have a solo practice, but you do not have to take care of every detail and task yourself. Let's look at a few items you can hand over to someone else. And before you go into a panic anxiety attack, I am not talking about hiring a staff member.

1) Your phones - What is your hourly rate? $125-300 per hour? Would you pay a receptionist this amount to answer your phone? H*** NO! That is exactly what you are doing when you answer them yourself, that is exactly what it is costing you each time you answer your phones. You are throwing away money and time. For a fraction of the cost, you can hire a receptionist firm to handle your incoming calls 24 hours a day. They are trained, specifically in the legal field. They are highly professional, can schedule appointments, respond to your online chat, and answer non-legal questions for you. A missed call costs you money and an answered call costs a lot when you are the one answering.

2) Find a good Virtual Assistant - You may have to interview a few to find the right fit for you and your firm but do it. You will thank me later. They handle all the tasks that are not billable. If a task is non-billable you should not be doing it anyway. A VA will handle anything from administrative tasks to marketing, social media, bookkeeping, updating your web site, research, and much more. Again for pennies on the dollar.

3) Get a paralegal - With more and more people working remotely, many firms have shut down, and paralegals are out of work. You can hire one on a contract basis (No benefit expense). They can work with you in the office or by remote.

The advantage of finding these services is that you do not have to pay the overhead you have with full-time employees, such as unemployment insurance, workers comp, medical insurance, 401K, etc.

Now you have the help you need at a fraction of the cost for you to do the work yourself. This frees you to be a lawyer in your solo firm and not everything else. Which is what you wanted to be.

How do you know what tasks to delegate? Anything that is not billable. Anything that does not involve giving legal advice.

I understand that there are some upfront costs that may hurt a little, but in the long run, you will increase your client intake, your leads, decrease you, no-shows, increase your retaining, and have more successful case conclusions, which lead to happy clients, client referrals, and good reviews. You can do this. You will find you have freed up time in your schedule to complete your work, have more personal time, and maybe even see the weekend or a sunset.

If you feel stuck, if the thought of setting all of this up is sending you into a panic attack then contact me. I can help you. We will create a plan, a road map, to make this into workable, not overwhelming, steps.

We will meet once a week over a 6-month period to create the practice that really works for you.

Together we will:
* Organize your schedule and to-do lists.
* Create more time in your workweek.
* Find the best help you need so you have time to focus on legal and not administrative tasks.
* Create more leads, retentions, and fewer no-shows.
* Improve your online presence.
* Experience dinners at home and weekends.
* Create a tailor-made plan.
* Have a high level of accountability to achieve your dream.

CHAPTER 11: Medium to Large Firm Attorneys

A friend or co-worker may have handed you this book. You thought it was rather good and contained good information. But you work for a larger firm. You have several attorneys and many paralegals and administrative help on the staff. How can this apply to you?

If you see your section or division as your own "law firm" these practices can apply. Do not try to reform the whole practice, just your corner of it.

For example, you are in a Personal Injury law firm and you handle all the motorcycle cases, while another handle falls, and another handles maritime injuries. You will work with your section of motorcycles.

You have your area in the office with your paralegals, legal assistance and maybe even an administrative assistant. This is your personal space and what you can work with. You can have a strong team, a fulfilling mission, and work from your core values.

Everything we have talked about earlier in this book would not apply to you. You can build an A+ team, have excellent client service, and a loyal clientele. Just do not think so big.

The nice thing with improving your corner of the firm is that this can have a positive effect on the other areas of the firm as well. When they see your team working as a strong cohesive unit. When the partners and other associates see the referrals and reviews improving, they may ask you, "What is your secret?" now wouldn't that feel good?

When you develop a team that you have such strong confidence in others will notice. When you can handle your case load and be home for dinners and important events, others will notice.

Many young attorneys must struggle with long hours, tight deadlines, and high pressure demands. This can literally make or break a lawyer, or their relationships.

It is my goal to teach strategies to help you thrive in the field of your dreams and be able to have a life as well. The secret is to be able to have a strong team behind you. Becoming known as an expert in your field. (This is easier than you think.) In a field that is already flooded with strong competition.

If you had read through all the previous material and thought it really did not apply to you because you are part of a larger firm, think again. We just need to rethink and reposition how you see yourself and your staff.

Maybe you began with a large firm, but your true dream is to work at a small or boutique firm, or even as a solo practitioner. You chose the large firm because you have student loans to pay and need the clientele that a large firm generates. We can work together to help you reach that goal.

Either way, we can plot out your goals and make the reachable for you. Remember the final goal is to work a profession that has been a long time coming and have a life you have always envisioned having.

Part 2: Your Personal Life

Why would I create a whole section in this book about you? Because this is your practice and your world. In business, everything trickles down from the top. If you do not have yourself in order, you will never have your business and your staff in order.

You went to college, passed the bar exam, and had a dream. How close are you to reaching that dream? If it still seems out of reach, then we will look at the work / life balance. Why you do what you do and how to make it a life that you love living.

If all you are doing is working and not living, enjoying your family and nurturing relationships outside of work, then it is time to work on you.

In this section, we will learn to integrate the best possible life mindset and practices, so you have a balanced life, and you do not feel like you are sacrificing personal time for work or work time for family.

CHAPTER 12: How to Create More Hours in you Day

How many times have you said, "I don't have enough time"? If you strip certain things out of your day or should I say daily habits, you will find that you do have more time.

Here are some questions for you to think about:

- Do you keep your cell phone on your desk?
- How many times a day do you check your work email?
- How many times a day do you check your personal email?
- How many times a day are you interrupted by unscheduled calls?
- Is your office flooded with paperwork? What if I asked you to send me pictures of your workspace right now? Being unorganized affects your time as well.
- Do you take any breaks during the day?
- Do employees come to your door to ask questions?

Your schedule

Who controls your schedule? You may think of your legal assistant, but you are wrong. You must control your schedule. If you feel you need more time in your day or even your week, then you can make it happen. At the law firm I work for, my boss sized down his availability for initial consultations to 3-days a week. He now works two days a week remotely. And we are thriving more than ever. We have strict rules about phone calls and appointments. Never a same-day appointment, and the only calls that he is told about while the person is on the phone will be a judge, lawyer, the IRS, and family (which is rare). All other calls go to voice mail or an email message.

With this type of scheduling guidelines, he can focus on the work in front of him. We are a small firm of seven employees, yet we bring in over 1 million a year in new business.

Your phone

Everyone has one; I have two; one for business and one for personal. I do keep my phones on my desk, but I have the sound turned down, and they sit face down, so I do not see every email, call, and notification. I have set with my family the times to call me. I just do not answer other times. Usually, it is at lunch and 4 pm during my commute home, since my car provides hands-free talking. I will check my emails and notifications during lunch or my breaks, but I do not answer them then. I save those for later in the day when I am at home relaxing.

I talk much more in-depth in a later chapter about phones. So here I am just touching on the basics. We all know the talk, but when you look around you, people are all either staring at a screen or having an electronic conversation with someone. Tell me if I am wrong. Look into a restaurant, and you will see what I mean. People out in public are all staring at their phones. People used to strike up conversations with those sitting next to them. Now they avoid each other by keeping the phones active.

I am extremely comfortable with talking with people I do not know. If you have met me at a convention or networking event, you will know what I am describing. I love to be able to say something to make people smile. I guess that is why I got into the study of psychology. I love people. I want to know what makes them tick. Why are people happy or sad? You cannot learn about people if you do not honestly talk with them and listen to them.

Virtual talk is not reliable communication. People think because others are hiding behind a screen that they let their guard down and are more honest. Well, this is not true for the majority because most people now days do not know the real art of communication, sharing, and listening (Hearing what is really said). You cannot do this on a smartphone, tablet, or computer.

During your workday, set the phone aside. You will be amazed at how many more minutes or even hours in your day when you are not constantly checking it.

Turn off your notifications from all the apps. You will be amazed at the minimum distractions you now have. I found that most of my notifications were people trying to sell an online seminar or class. Now I choose when to go into my apps and see what is going on with friends and family. I am doing it on my terms and in my time.

Your emails

In the books I have read, and the conferences I have attended on time management and productivity, email is called a time vampire. I agree. We waste a lot of time on it. If you have a filtering tool in your email, then direct emails to specific folders based on who it is from or keywords. That way, those emails are organized for the time set aside to work on that person or topic.

I have one folder for all clients that I need to contact to schedule appointments. I know that I make my calls in the afternoon. I do not even look at that folder until then. If I do, then I will have other things on my mind, and I am not productively working on what I should focus on right now. I have another folder for leads, another for my marketing tasks. First thing in the morning, I go through my inbox and organize items into folders so I can work on them at a designated time. Or even a day. I update all my reporting on Friday, just like I know I will be assisting the front office with the phones on Mondays. I do not focus those days on my busy direct mail tasks.

I do not check all emails as soon as they hit my screen. But I do get a flash of what comes in. Now for the bosses and attorneys. You can turn off your emails when working on an important project. Hopefully, you have already put email times on your schedule. Those are the times of the days that you devote to check, responding, or delegating emails.

For the busier people, you can even have a staff person who checks your emails for you. They can weed out the spam, and those emails that do not need your attention. I would say a good number of the emails you get from clients can be answered by the paralegals who are handling the cases. New inquiries for service can be turned over to marketing or intake. You are not making money by giving free advice. It is also ethically irresponsible to answer the legal questions outside of a full consultation. If it is your field of law and the person lives in your service area, then they need a meeting, send that to intake or the receptionist to follow up and set an appointment.

Your time to work... Uninterrupted

Sometimes you need to shut your door, place your phone on Do Not Disturb, shut down the interoffice messenger and text program, and just get work done. Make sure all your staff understands your uninterrupted time. If that does not seem to be happening, then remove yourself from the office. You can work from home or go to a library. Anywhere you can feel undistracted. Make this time a habit. You will get so much done in much shorter time frames. If you need your office for the files and reference materials, be sure your staff respects your time and space.

Thinking you need more time is irrelevant. Make the time. Reorder your priorities, shut off the sound on your phone, turn off your email, remote work one or two days a week. Being unorganized in space and mind is a huge time waste. There are ways to create more hours in your work week without stealing more time away from your personal life.

Time is what we want most,
but use the worst.

~ William Penn

CHAPTER 11: A Work-Life Balance

We do not live so we can work, we work so we can live.

Business comes and goes. It is a struggle to start new, and then there are slumps in business. You need to be bringing in the revenue to make payroll and pay office expenses, not to mention your salary and bills. If you are working yourself to exhaustion, straining your relationships, and not taking some time for your peace of mind, what are you working to achieve in your life? How do you strike that balance and make all your hard work worth it?

You might think that your only choice is to bring work home with you, or just devoting a few more hours a week will help you jump the hurdle in front of you. But what is happening? You start to get stressed and tired. You are taking away from your family time, putting stress and strain on your work, your relationships, and probably your health. This is so counter-intuitive. But you feel you need to devote more time. And I understand that some things require this but not consistently. You have an emergency, or a big trail is coming up, it is the end of tax season, etc. Making this a regular habit, though, will leave you alone and your life empty.

I restrict myself to a certain number of work hours a week. When I am at those hours, I stop. Sometimes my workload is more substantial than others, but I still manage to get all that work done within the allotted hours. I just set my priorities, reschedule my workflow, set a realistic deadline, and delegate where appropriate. Working more just creates a situation where you are no longer nice to be around, your thinking is impaired, exhausted, feeling guilty because of the lack of family time or feeling run down and possibly sick.

I cannot say that I do not think about work when I am at home, but I take a realistic view that I really cannot do anything about it right now. So, I focus on my family and that they are the reason I am working so hard. Have I spent time talking with my son today? Did I ask my husband about his day and REALLY listen to his sharing? I know I am the one person who will listen to anything he has to share and be unconditional with him. Did we get out and do something not work-related during our time off?

Let us Talk Phones

Even at home, I have strict personal phone guidelines. They are either turned off or left in another room at dinner. Well, honestly, my phones are almost always in my bedroom. I tap the screen when I walk by just to see what notifications there are. But then unless something needs my attention during my time, then I will check later. I have found that if I have my phones with me, I will keep checking them.

We are kind of a lazy family. We eat in front of the TV. Yes, almost every day. But we do not have our phones. We spend this time together. My policy is that I never answer my phone when it rings unless we are working with a crisis. If the call is important, the caller will leave a message. I leave most of my non-business phone calls for the weekend. It is not fair to my friends and family to be rushed through a conversation because I need to run into a meeting or even get dinner out of the oven.

I remember the day that the only phone you had was sitting on your desk or hanging on the kitchen wall. We did not even have answering machines yet. But we managed fine, we communicated even more. Or at least, more real. The world will not end if you are driving down the road, not having a conversation with someone. We are so attached to our devices. We are losing sight of the people right in front of us. The ones that really matter.

What about your family?

Make your kids' events a priority. Does your son have a soccer game, your daughter a recital? Be sure to place these on your work calendar. Do not schedule anything during those times. If you are thinking, "Well, I can miss this one time and go to the next one." There may not be a next one. Nothing in life is guaranteed. One thing I have learned from being a mother and a counselor is you cannot disappoint your children. They will quickly learn that your word is not good, and they cannot rely on you to be their biggest fan. Words are never enough.

These children are brilliant, and actions are what they hear. If you love them, you must show it. Be there for them. The first 18 years fly by so fast, and you cannot recapture lost moments. Remember why you are working so hard? It is for them. It is also so you can enjoy the special moments in their life with them. Remember, they will become the husbands, wives, and parents that you set as an example for them.

If you have a significant other, husband, wife, whatever, then be sure to plan a regular "Date Night." It does not have to be elaborate or expensive. It just must be time spent together. I do this with my kids also. Individually, so I am focusing on just them. Often a lunch date on the weekend. You get one chance in life to build these relationships. Time goes so fast, and this is one thing you cannot put off. If you cannot afford date nights, then give me a quick shout out, and I will throw some great ideas your way. You have worked hard for your relationships. You need to spend time nurturing them even when you feel your plate is full. Go out with your wife, husband, or partner and leave your phones on silent. Try your best not to look at them unless you are making sure the babysitter is not calling. If you are going out to a restaurant, just give the babysitter the restaurant number in case of an emergency. Then you will have an hour or two hours to spend with the person you love.

You work long and hard so that you can have the life of your dreams. Chances are the vision you had, included your family. If your whole life becomes work to provide for them, the dream is not achieved. You must strike that healthy balance. You will find you are more productive at work and less distracted, which equals more getting accomplished in less time, and you make more money so you can enjoy your family more and reach your dreams.

If this is truly a challenge for you, then a life coach may be a good idea. It is often a good idea to have an objective personal trainer to help you reorder your priorities.

What are you doing for you?

If you are not careful, you will find that every moment of your day is filled up, and not with the things you would enjoy doing. You end up on that hamster wheel of getting up, being busy with work, running errands, dinner, stuff you need to do at home, and then bed. Just to get up and do it all over again the next day. What do you do for yourself to slow down a little and have some time to relax and breath? If your whole life is filled with busy work, you will lose your mind.

I get up 30-minutes before everyone else. Having quiet time allows me to have coffee, listen to my daily motivation, and just wake up. I started doing this when my kids were in school. I quickly learned that as soon as they are up, the whirlwind would hit. By getting up that extra 30-minutes, I was able to begin my day with peace and quiet and set my spirit right where it needs to be.

Do you have a hobby? Do you like to read, learn something new, make something with your hands, or possibly just throw the pole in the water? Everyone needs something that lets them escape the every day for just a little while. Doing something that has nothing to do with your everyday can be refreshing and give you a greater sense of self-expression and self-awareness. Maybe you want to go for a run, work out, meditate, play a video game, write in a journal, or go fishing. Everyone has their pastime that feeds their soul and keeps them connected to themselves.

Staying on top of your stuff is important. Do not let the mess build up around you. Is your car clean, is your house is neat, do you have an organized office? Organization is something to keep up with every day. It takes so little time to put things away right away and keep things organized. If you are not, then your life has fallen out of balance. By staying on top of things that potentially become a mess, it takes a lot less time than having to sort it, organize, and clean up the messes later.

Do you get 8-hours of sleep a night? You may be thinking, how would that be possible in my life? Well, if you make it a priority, you will find yourself more energized, focused, and productive during your working hours. It sounds like you are taking away from possible work time, but by being rested, you are creating more time because you get more accomplished in less time.

There is a feature on iPad that let you set a timer 30 minutes before bed, and then you hear the alarm 8-hours later. It is an excellent tool. When you hear the chime that tells you it is 30 minutes to bedtime, get ready for bed. Remember to spend a few minutes being grateful for your day to set your night right. More about that later.

These four primary things that can keep you centered. You will be more "THERE" for your family and your work. You will find you are better rested, have a more apparent peace of mind, you will have better health, and have good relationships with friends, family, and coworkers.

We think, mistakenly, that success is the result of the amount of time we put in at work, instead of the quality of time we put in.

~Arianna Huffington

Chapter 14: Eliminate, Delegate or Automate

These steps sound easy to do, and they really make a lot of sense, but sometimes it is much easier to think about a process than to do it. Implementing these steps for some can be planned over a weekend. You could be one of those action-oriented people who sit down and restructure because you see the benefit. Others are intimidated with change and can use a coach to help restructure. A fresh set of eyes can help you know what your possibilities and opportunities are.

Let me go through these quickly to give you some ideas that will free up time for you and your staff. They can also create a higher flow of potential clients, new clients, and revenue growth.

Eliminate the Extra

There are so many areas and ways that professionals take on way too much. In business, we learned from a young age that to succeed, we must work hard. If we were not busy, then we were lazy, or a well-known saying, "No Pain, No Gain."

I am telling you now. We were all sold a lie. Filling every moment with busy work is not a sign of good productivity. It is a way to fill the time, and that is it. If you give an employee 8-hours, they will find a way to fill the 8-hours. If you give them a 4-hour deadline, they will get the same amount of work completed and probably do a better job at it.

Many times, we put things on our to-do list that really are not necessary. Phone calls can be handled by email and many tasks can be accomplished by others—or even many items can be eliminated.

So, let us eliminate unneeded items from your firm, your work list, and your weekly calendar.

Do you practice in a niche market? Everyone knows that word by now. Do you have a single focus in a single market, or are you a jack of all trades? Are you chasing dollars or working from passion?

As a law firm, you need a narrower focus. You need to be an expert in your field. Where does your passion lie? What are your strengths? If you work as a general practitioner, then you are most likely spread too thin. If you try to be good at everything, you will not excel at anything.

Do you take anyone as a client out of fear of empty calendar space or lack of funds? A lead comes in, and they do not feel like a good fit for you or your firm. You just know this is someone who will be demanding, needy, or asking more than they are worth. But they can pay the full retainer, you need the money, and what if more leads do not call right away?

You cannot run your practice out of fear. When the perfect clients show up, you are now too busy or tired to serve them or at least serve them well. You can choose your ideal clients and be selective. Know who your perfect client is. Have referral sources for those you do not wish to represent.

I was talking with an attorney recently that has a solo practice. She was telling me about a client that was more work than she was worth. The attorney was overworked. I told her to find a new client at the same amount and refund the trouble client. She told me she needed the next one just to pay the mortgage. How could she refund a client when the money was used on bills? I told her to go and find two new clients who are a better fit for the practice. Having one troublesome client will take all your time, energy, and cost you more in the long run. Was it worth taking them on just to have one more on the books? They are not profitable. Cut your losses and turn away those who are not a good fit.

Now let us talk about meetings. We have always seen meetings as a part of business. But do you know how much those meetings cost you? Say you have a weekly meeting with some of your staff. They are not working on cases now, so no billable hours. When a session starts, how quickly do you get down to business, or how long do you spend talking about things that are not on the list like the associate's sons little league game? What are you covering in the meeting collectively? Are these items that can be handled quicker one-on-one, or through an email message? How necessary is the session you are holding? If they are not, then do not schedule them.

If you must have a meeting, create a list ahead of time and email to the participants. When they come, they are expected to be prepared and get right to the list. Do not waste time. That extra 45 minutes could mean you are getting home for dinner tonight, or not.

At the beginning of your week, make a list of all the priority to-do items for the next week. The list will include important projects, phone calls, and meetings. Take a realistic look at the list and see what is needed to be accomplished by you. Your list of weekly priorities should only contain about three items. Everything else can either be eliminated or delegated.

Delegate

We all know the word, but it seems hard to do. If you give that important project to someone else, they may not do as good a job on it. Do you trust your staff? Did you hire them to fill chairs, or are they qualified to get things accomplished and accomplished well? Hopefully, it is the later.

What are you taking on that is not worth your $300+ per hour fee? Most client inquiries, a paralegal can handle and new prospects by the front office. There is a big chunk of your phone messages and emails taken off your list.

What are some of the things, as a business owner, you are taking care of that you should not?

- Answering the phone
- Sorting email and mail.
- Answering most emails from clients and prospects.
- Working on your firm's social media
- Writing blog posts
- Preparing PowerPoint for a meeting or speaking engagement
- Your bookkeeping.
- The list goes on

Learning to delegate is a big step. The rewards are endless, though. If you label tasks with a price tag, you can free up a lot of your time and your budget.

In your practice, can you free up tasks by outsourcing? Outsourced tasks can be anything from the receptionist to bookkeeping to marketing. These were a traditionally full-time position that now can be handled by an outsourcing service part-time and at great savings to you.

In our firm, we always answered the phone. We loved the personal touch. A full-time employee (the receptionist) would answer every call. We switched to a VOIP service with individual voice mail that transcribed to email. Each call went directly to the person needed. At the beginning of the call is a message of how to go online to schedule a free consultation. Online scheduling has become popular with new prospects.

We eliminated the receptionist and have just the front office manager. By not having the constant interruption of the phones, one person was able to absorb the vacant position.

As the business owner, you do not have the $12+ per hour for 40 hour a week but also the benefits that cost you as well. (Medical, Dental, Unemployment, workers comp etc.)

We had a part-time bookkeeper that spent more time shopping online than keeping the books. She did not bring in any profit to the firm. We moved to QuickBooks, and having an outsourced bookkeeper come in twice a month to reconcile the books. The front office brought in all money from clients and posted them, and bills paid out were recorded at the time payment is made.

Many marketing tasks can also be outsourced. There are so many programs to create leads, follow-up, and automate. I almost hate to write about this because I can practically eliminate my position as the Marketing Director at my firm.

Marketing items that can be outsourced:

- Your intake can be automated.
- Your leads
- Your scheduling and confirming appointments
- Client tasks, follow-up, collections, and reviews.
- Even my direct mail marketing lists can be outsourced to a data entry service and sent directly to the printers to produce the letters and mail out.

Automation in Business

It is remarkable the products and programs in place today. You can set up a campaign series and it communicates and generates for you. All you need is the simple input in the beginning. It will direct contact and communications based on the actions prospects and clients take or do not take.

Let me give you an example.

An inquiry either calls the intake person or fills out a form online.

A lead is created.

They receive an email letting them know how to schedule a free consultation

They receive a confirmation the day before or day of the appointment.

They have an appointment.

They receive an email on how to retain and pay.

Or:

They cancel or are a no-show, they get an email of how to reschedule.

Or:

They should but did not hire

They receive instruction on how to have further questions answered.

Or:

They hired - They get instructions on how to deliver documents securely online.

Clients are discharged - they receive a review request.

Automation is a stable part of the business. It is a wonderful analysing tool, as well. Every program out there creates reports for you to follow the path of engagement with prospects and clients.

It may take an initial investment of money and time to create, but once you have it in place, it runs itself. You can even outsource the creation of your campaigns. You just need to create the original materials that will go into your campaigns.

When you have automation in place, you have your business running 24-hours a day.

I will give you an example of one of my coaching practices. I have my blogs and newsletters. I write them at my convenience, and they are scheduled to publish at a certain day and time. I can write several in one day and have them cover a month of communicating with my clients. I could even outsource the writing to a copywriting firm for a reasonable cost and save myself time. There are links in everything I publish for prospects to schedule a free consultation, and the series begins.

Once they schedule a second appointment, they are led to the payment portal after they schedule that appointment, CRM delivers content to engage people and keep in contact. (CRM - Client Relationship Management Software)

A person reads an article that inspires them to learn more. They read about my 60-day course. They click the link to schedule for the group course. When they finish scheduling, they are sent to the payment portal. After they make a payment, they are provided information on how to find the course, the video conferences, schedule one-on-one time, and downloads.

All of this is set up once and keeps working over and over, 24 hours a day, seven days a week, 365 days a year.

I do not need a receptionist to field calls, or marketing people to follow up, or instructors to teach unless I want them for the live sessions.

Let us do the math.

Scheduling program costs $15+ / month

CRM and campaigns $50+ / Month

There are many programs out there that offer the full services through integration. You can have a scheduling program that also works as a CRM and is linked with your payment portal.

Under $100 per month, I have an automated system in place. Now the larger the list of contacts you have, the more it can cost, but the numbers still work in your favour.

A receptionist at $12/ hour not including benefits $1920/month

Marketing $30/per hour $4800/month

Teaching $250/hour at 8 hours a month $2000

For a fraction of the cost, you can hire freelancers to create, connect, and automate what you are paying full-time staff to do, or using your own time to do. You now can have one person in the office to do the work of 2-3 people. This person can give a personal touch with clients, to field your emails, so you do not have to spend a couple of hours a day moving them around or answering them. You only get the ones that need your attention. Can you automate much of what your staff is currently doing?

Another advantage of today's technology is remote working. We have a paralegal that works from home 2-days a week and has three days in the office so she can have appointments to file cases. Our lead attorney works from home two days a week and comes in 3 days for consultations. When the front office manager is at home, she can respond to client requests, schedule appointments, and even take and return phone calls through her cell phone with the office phone number showing as the caller id. You could eliminate the need for large, expensive office space, allow flex time working, and still give great service to your clients. If approved by your bar association, the courts and judges, many client contacts can even be handled remotely through FaceTime, Skype, Zoom, and other video conferencing services. Video conferencing may be a good consideration with the onset of COVID-19 and the need for people to be home with their kids (schools closed) or just keeping clients safer by letting them meet with you from home. I put thought into this with the rise of the virus. We can, as a firm, do just as well if we are confined to home. It would not be difficult with today's technology.

Could you imagine what your work week would look like if you can practice from home? You could video conference your staff meetings, client meetings, filings, and other appointments. You would still need to go to court, mediations, and depositions, but you could spend more time in the comfort of your home. Remote work would cut out commutes, tolls, and gas expenses as well. One of the nicest benefits is you could be at the dinner table with your family every night at 5 or 6 pm.

The Future of working.

The coaching field already works highly automated. Many service fields are shifting. Automation frees up your time to help more people, focus better in your one-on-one time, and increase the number of people you can serve. We as coaches, can now work with an international clientele where we were once limited to local clients only. It also frees up time for speaking, writing, and other aspects of the business we did not previously have time to pursue.

I know this can be confusing. The first half of the book focused on staff. Having the best team possible to wow your clients and make you more money. The second half focuses on streamlining your work and eliminating unneeded staff. We are looking at a transformation of how we conduct business. Even more importantly, we look at a shift in the perspective of being able to reach your dreams without killing your spirit. Life is meant to be lived and lived with those we love, while at the same time pursuing your purpose and passion.

No matter how you restructure your business, you will still need paralegals and front office staff of some kind. The people you have in place is vitally important to your success. Remember, though, that all progress and great work environment starts at the top and trickle down. Everything begins with you. What are your core values? How do you communicate these to your staff and clients? What makes you stand out from the crowd? If family and life is a priority, you can position yourself as the CEO of your firm and not be so hands-on with the day-to-day running of your firm.

Do you want the time and freedom to take a family vacation? How about one without your phone and laptop? Would you enjoy being at home most nights to have dinner with your family?

What is it you want? Why did you start reading this book? How about no more 12-hour days? How about a 5-day work week with weekends off?

What you want can only be created by you. The first thought is usually all the objections.

I cannot do that because…

Let us play a game. Write down all your objections. All the reasons you cannot free up more time. Remember, you already have the A+ staff. They will be on your side of creating a better work-life balance for yourself. With your example, they can do this for themselves as well. All while generating higher profits and happy clients.

Let us look at the objections

- Your staff needs you there to get the work done.
- Only you can handle A, B, or C.
- Keep going…

You will see that most of what you list are old and often misguided beliefs.

As you begin to see, there is a better way to work; your beliefs begin to shift. You only need a 1% shift in thinking to steer toward a completely new destination.

Would it surprise you or hurt your feelings to know that you do not have to stand over your staff's shoulder for work to get completed promptly? I hope not. If you have clear expectations and trust in your team, the job gets done, even when you are there or not.

You do not need to be the one who handles all the business. Keep looking at your list of priorities and responsibilities and see what you can eliminate, delegate, or automate. You will be amazed how much gets accomplished when you direct staff to work for focused and tighter deadlines. People fill the time they have. Remember, an 8-hour project can be completed, often even better, if given a 4-hour deadline.

Are you the one who conducts every consultation, goes to every hearing, signs all documents, handles every email and phone call? If you are, you will never see the light of day.

You can hire an associate to handle all hearing. Leaving court to someone else allows you free to be at the consultations, and schedule more of them. The office can handle most emails and phone calls. I know paralegals hate the phone, but many questions can be managed directly from them. Block out calendar times for them to focus on returning phone calls. Most client emails do not need your attention. Any client communication can be blocked out in certain time frames.

Are you working on bringing in leads and following up until they retain? Your front office can do this or even better, these steps can be automated.

You can practice law, run your firm, and have the life of your dreams, all at the same time. You do not have to work yourself into an early grave. You do not have to sacrifice your family and relationships to be successful as a lawyer.

What you must do is believe it before you see it. It will take work in the beginning and commitment from everyone on your team. But this is a very realistic dream being reached by lawyers across the country.

Imagine next year. You are spending more time with your family, in two years the profits are growing, in three you are thriving in your practice and your personal life.

"Marketing automation allows law firms to do what has previously been nearly impossible: Deliver the RIGHT MESSAGE to the RIGHT CLIENT at the RIGHT TIME."

~ Michelle Calcote King

Part 3: Thriving Through Drastic Changes

"We must adjust to changing times and still hold to unchanging principles."

~ Jimmy Carter

Chapter 15: How the World has Changed

When I first started writing this book, I had no idea what was coming. No one did. With the outbreak and worldwide spread of the coronavirus, the world and how we work in it has changed. At first, I was a little upset because I thought that this book was obsolete. As I thought about it, though, I realize this book and what we speak of here, is more relevant than ever before.

Are you looking at your firm dwindling as a quoted "non-essential business"? With the stay-at-home orders, your staff has been scattered to the wind. The world has changed, and many are waiting for the virus to pass so we can get back to normal. The important thing to realize right now is that the normal we once knew will never come back. We are evolving, and we will come out of all of this with a new normal.

So, let us talk about how you can survive as a law practice and even better how to thrive through the changes we are expecting and not expecting. Instead of fearing the future, law firms can forge ahead with a new level of service. The opportunity to stand out in your field is greater than ever before.

Many of the things you need to do to thrive have already been discussed in previous chapters. What I want to do here is take away some of the fear, confusion, and open your eyes to clarity in uncertain times.

The one thing we have seen is that the law has not stopped. People still need lawyers, and lawyers still need their staff. Injuries still occur. People need help with unemployment, divorce, bankruptcy, immigration, etc. We are a service-based industry, and that is our strength, we are still greatly needed.

Right now, even more than ever, having the right people working for you in place is more critical than ever. People are frightened, uncertain, and scared of what the future brings. Law Offices can provide direction, reassurance, and help people in these troubling times. Remember than in every interaction you make is a potential client or referral source.

Your Office

You had to close your doors, not only because the states ordered it, but to keep yourself and your staff safe and healthy. Closing your doors does not mean you cannot practice just as you were before. With the ability of remote working there is no need to miss a beat. By making sure that every staff member can work remotely. Every file, every calendar, and every program used in the office is still available to you and your staff.

Not only are the computers remote, so are the phones. There is no reason to miss a single call. IT can set up apps where the office phones are set to your cell phones by extension. Clients are now directed exactly to the team member they need. The voice messaging system has streamlined the calling process. Clients do not have to go through a receptionist to speak to the paralegals or attorneys. The phones, if not answered, will email a transcribed message. You do not have to answer every call when they come in. You can stick to your commitment of only speaking to clients on the phone at specific times. Also, as an attorney, remember what your time is worth. You can forward the client calls to the paralegals who are handling their case and scheduling and retaining calls to the intake person.

An important note about hiring IT. There are companies out there that specialize in law firms. They know the needs and the programs that law firms use. This is recommended.

Managing Your Team.

There will always be the one person on your team that will think working remotely means they can catch up on their latest Netflix Binge. Managing your organization can be easy.

1) Set your expectations at the beginning. Time billing and other features allow you to see how productive a person is.

   (As marketing, I do not use time billing, but I keep my accountability by keeping a daily list of everything I need to do, and I check it off as I get tasks completed. My list is sent to my boss at the end of every day. He knows what I have accomplished during any given day. The list also cuts down on his need to ask if tasks are achieved. I am saving him time. This list also keeps him informed of upcoming consultations and filing appointments.)

"To successfully work with other people, you have to trust each other. A big part of this is trusting people to get their work done wherever they are, without supervision."

~ Sir Richard Branson

2) Set communication expectations. It is more important than ever to be communicating with your clients. A short phone call can set someone's mind at ease much quicker than an email or text. People are cut off from each other, and they do not know the changes taking place. Speaking with the clients helps them feel confident in your professional approach to stay-home-orders and to manage their cases. Be proactive. Do not wait for them to call. Have the front office and paralegals reach out to clients and reassure them that you are taking care of them.

2) On your web site, on the home page, put a statement or link where people can get information about how your firm is working in this new time. The statement will eliminate the need for extra calls and emails of people asking questions that can easily be answered on your web site.

3) Have a 15-minute weekly staff meeting. Either by conference call or group video. Both are easy to set up and can be free. Through programs like Zoom video, you can meet and check-in with each other through video or a service like freeconferencecalling.com you can set the conference phone meetings.

Hopefully, you have already established the A+ team by the ideas set forth earlier in this book. If you have that level of teamwork, there should be little to manage as we enter this new era of business.

Electronic Documents

One thing that attorneys do not often think about is the number of documents your staff needs to handle to prepare and file a case. During this time of virus protection, it is important to communicate to your clients that documents need to be delivered electronically. This is a good practice to begin, establish and keep with even after the COVID-19 scare is over. It is just a healthy habit for those people who must handle all that paperwork.

The documents can be scanned and sent by email, uploaded to your programs, you can use google docs, drop box and many other services to keep the transfer of sensitive information secure, all the while looking out for the health and safety of your staff.

Managing your Clients

You should have already established a client communication protocol. Creating a communication contract with your clients that they sign allows them to know how your firm communicates with clients, and how you expect clients to communicate with the office. If you have certain days and times that you reply to emails or return phone calls, it may be good to re-establish these terms with your clients. It is important not to change how you operate just because your locations have changed.

People feel the need for reassurance and communications right now. Set your boundaries early to avoid unneeded time wasters in your days. Your staff will get quite a few calls from clients that are looking to see how things have changed. How are the hearings being conducted, how are appointments now handled?

You can send out an initial email using your regular client mailing list to inform everyone at the same time. The downside of this is all companies are emailing COVID-19 updates and people are not opening these emails as much anymore. You can also send a mailing to all clients. Not everyone will read when you mail or email but enough will so that it cuts down on the number of calls the office will receive.

Stick to your schedule, maintain your routine, and take advantage of the free time you do have.

Managing Yourself

I still work 8-5. I get up in the morning, have my coffee, take time to meditate and journal then get ready for work. I always dress for work. Preparing for the day helps me to be in the right frame of mind to be professional. Keeping the routines helps to stay on track. What I do not have any more is the commute. I have an extra two hours in my day that I did not have before.

The one thing that most people complained about previously was they did not have enough time. Now everyone has been allotted more time. Prayers answered, Right? Find something you enjoy doing that is not work. Take some time to relax, work on a hobby, or play with your kids.

Stick to a schedule. If you have an office with doors, this is much easier. Set a schedule, communicate it, and stick to it. Outside of those hours, do not even enter the office. The draw of the computer in the other room can be strong. When you realize you forgot something, it is so easy to run in and get it done quickly. But doing something even quickly ends up being more hours working. I was speaking to an attorney the other day who told me he was working until 4 am. Do not fill your worry and anxiety with more hours of work.

Take time to do something you have always wanted to do. You have more free time. You may not have had free time in quite a while. Do you even know what to do with yourself? It is more challenging since we must stay home. If you do not find a productive use of the time you can get bored, fall into depression, or revert to your old habit, over-working. It is quite easy to work more and longer hours. The problem with that is you will exhaust yourself, burn out, and not to mention upset your family.

If you do not have a designated home office where you can close the doors after your workday, shut your computer completely down. Out if sight (Mostly) out of mind. If your work is sitting on a screen where you easily can see it then you are more likely to be drawn to it. This is a great time to develop new habits with your work and your professional life.

"One of the secret benefits of using remote workers is that the work itself becomes the yardstick to judge someone's performance."

~ Jason Fried

Some Recommended Technology

IT

If you do not have a smart and available IT company you can call to help you stay up to date, you need one. I know solopreneurs are more likely to try to handle everything themselves. If you can find one that is familiar with the legal field and legal software, you have found a gold mine. Your IT person can become the most valuable expense next to your marketing director. If you do not know of someone who knows the legal field and their software programs, ask around. Start with people who practice the same field of law you do. Some software programs are specific for your area of law, and some are general for any type of practice.

Phones

We hesitated for a long time switching to a VOIP phone system. Now I do not know why it took us so long. The VOIP allows for flexibility and freedom. When we knew the stay at home order was coming, we were able to have our office extensions switched to our cell phones using an app. Now when we call clients, they still get the office phone number and not our cell. You know they will try calling at 2 am. This way, you can turn off your phone sound after-hours also, no late-night calls. Voice mails transcriptions are sent to work email, so you do not miss a call.

We are getting New Clients – Yes, even now.

What you really want to know is how to get new clients even right now. It is possible. The key to bringing in new clients now or ever is in the follow-up. Legal situations have not stopped because of the virus. They may have slowed, but they do not go away.

If you have a newsletter, then continue to write and distribute it. If you have a blog post write pertinent yet interesting articles.

Ok, the key to creating new clients while attorneys may be scrambling, is in the follow-up, not just the people that contacted you in the last few days or week. You want to reach the out to people that had cancelled their appointments, the no-shows, and those who had initial consultations and have not yet hired you.

Communicating this way is not a hard sell to get them to retain. Contact people just to reach out. Let them know you are concerned about them and their legal situation. Has it been resolved? If not, then you have an opening to take another look. If these are people that have not retained the firm, then let them know how they can retain during the stay-at-home order.

Follow up is crucial even in the best of times. These are the people most likely to fall through the cracks. If you do not have a follow-up plan set, then you are losing many potential clients. If they choose to hire someone else, I just say to people, "I'm happy you found someone to help with your situations." I keep it short and sweet.

You may be thinking, "I don't have enough time to call all of these people." You do not have to do it personally. You can have a staff member work on this project. Just make sure it is one who has a kind and compassionate disposition. I do not recommend a paralegal because they are busy already, and there seems to be an aversion to phones for most paralegals.

An important thing to keep in mind is that not everyone hires an attorney right away. Some come back a year or two later. But by taking extra steps to make people feel cared about, they will most likely come back to you or at least refer you to a friend or family member.

Video Conferencing

The video technology available now is great. You do not need expensive hardware, software, or editing programs. I like is Zoom because that is what I have the most familiarity with. but there is also GoToMeeting, Skype, Facetime, Microsoft Teams, and many others that for a small amount you can use, some are even free.

Let me tell you why I like Zoom and you can try out different ones to see if they have the features you need. I started out with zoom for my coaching. You can invite more than one person into a video call. When you set it up, you can send the others an invite that is received in their email with instructions to click on a link to join a meeting. You can record your sessions, and you also have a screen share feature. The best thing about zoom is for the basic features, there is no cost. You can keep a more personal connection with clients because you can see them face to face. With the free feature, there is, I believe, a 45-minute time frame. Having a time frame limitation allows you to stay focused and on task.

I am not recommending one program over another. I suggest you try a few with friends or colleges and see which you like. I only have experience with zoom. It is easily available to everyone.

In Conclusion

I began writing this book about one year ago. I could never have imagined then what the world would be facing now. No one did. The fact is that we live in an ever-changing world. When I first started my corporate work back in the late 80, telephones still had wires; receptionists' hand-wrote messages, and people were smoking in the office. Our computer servers took a whole large room that we called a cold-room because they were huge and had needed to be kept at a cooler temperature. Faxes came through on curled thermal sheets. Typewriters were used more than computers. The world has gotten simpler and more complicated at the same time.

I guess my point is that there will always be changes in business. If you set your team up for success, set yourself and your practice, you can flow with the changes, and still survive and thrive.

I am sure there are many solo and small firms that may not survive the coronavirus. Not because employees get sick, but because they lacked the organization to keep the flow of clients coming in during the shift.

My goal is to help as many firms as I can not only survive the changes but to thrive in the changes.

Thank you for joining me.

I enjoyed writing this book. The world changed drastically during the time I spend writing. I hope you got a lot out of this information to make your firm, whether solo, small, or medium size, a top performer in your area. You should now have an A+ team in place running your practice like a well-oiled machine.

The goal in life is two-fold. Have a business that you are proud of and supports you and have an experience that is enjoyable with the people you love. As an attorney or any service industry leader, you can have both. Life is meant to be lived and be fun. Life is not about working to survive.

If you are interested in assistance and coaching to create the A+ office, or if you are needing help and assistance in finding that life balance, you can find me at https://www.ashleyjspurgeon.com/ I look forward to hearing from you. I am also available for speaking at company events and workshops.

Ashley J. Spurgeon

About the Author:

Hello,

I am Ashley Spurgeon. I live and work out of the Houston, Texas area. I was the Director of Marketing and Front Office Manager for a Houston Law Firm, for over 6 years where I developed a love for the legal field and those we serve. Along with my 30+ years in the business world, from corporate offices to working for myself, I have a wide range of experiences that I pull into my practice, speaking and writing. I am a wife, mother, sister, daughter, friend, and business owner/entrepreneur.

Also, a Life/Business coach, speaker, and author. Life can never bring too much. With my studies focused on Marketing Management and Psychology I found a beautiful combination for client satisfaction and connections in all my business endeavours. I hope you gleaned some helpful information from my sharing.

My passions are helping people to stretch themselves to be their best in all areas of life. As my mentor Les Brown says, "You've got to be hungry," to reach your dreams. The services I offer are personal coaching, business coaching, and speaking to groups and businesses. I offer live speaking engagements as well as virtual. Please contact me through my web site for dates available and rates.

Made in the USA
Middletown, DE
07 January 2023

18896294R00076